Eighteenth-Century Clothing at Williamsburg

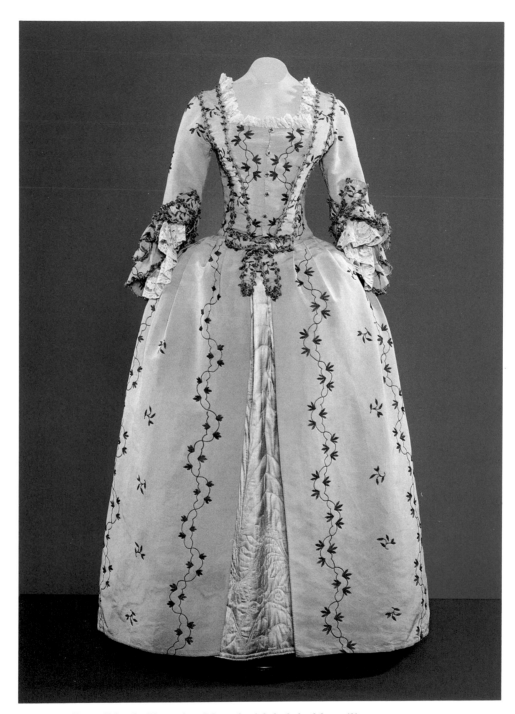

Gown. Yellow ribbed silk embroidered with bright blue silk,
linen bodice and sleeve linings, silk trim, England, 1770-1780.
The attached stomacher has nonfunctional buttons; the gown
fastens by hooks and eyes at the left front. 1953-850.

■ *A Wallace Gallery Decorative Arts Publication*

Eighteenth-Century Clothing at Williamsburg

by Linda Baumgarten

Introduction by Mildred B. Lanier

The Colonial Williamsburg Foundation
Williamsburg, Virginia

ISBN 0-87935-109-8

Printed in the United States of America

Library of Congress Cataloging-in-Publication Data

Baumgarten, Linda.
  Eighteenth-century clothing at Williamsburg.

  (Williamsburg decorative arts series)
    1. Costume — Virginia — History — 18th century — Catalogs.
  2. Costume — History — 18th century — Catalogs. 3. DeWitt Wallace
  Gallery of Decorative Arts — Catalogs. I. DeWitt Wallace Gallery of
  Decorative Arts. II. Title. III. Series.
  GT617.V8B38 1986   391'.009755   86-20726
  ISBN 0-87935-109-8

Foreword

WITH the opening of the DeWitt Wallace Decorative Arts Gallery in 1985, Colonial Williamsburg is able to exhibit more of its extensive collections of seventeenth-, eighteenth-, and early nineteenth-century English and American arts than ever before. The Wallace Gallery has made it possible for us to set the objects seen in the exhibition buildings in the Historic Area of the restored eighteenth-century city of Williamsburg — the capital of the largest British colony in North America — in the context not just of one particular place at quite specific times but rather of the colonies in general as an integral part of the British Empire. By comparing the material aspects of life in and around Williamsburg with London, or Edinburgh, or Charleston, South Carolina, for example, we are able to get a clearer idea of what distinguished this place from others in the period and what were common characteristics of many of them. As the collections here at Williamsburg have grown progressively more encyclopedic (in their particular genre), so it has become more and more possible to make comparisons not only of place but also of time — the mid-seventeenth century compared to the mid-eighteenth century, for example — as well as of social type — objects reserved for the affluent versus those relegated to the middle classes. Obviously, this contributes an extra dimension to the educational experiences we can offer our visitors.

And our visitors include those with wide-ranging general interests as well as specialists.

It therefore behooves us to make available published records of our collections and the fruits of our ongoing research in ways that appeal to both groups. We have in the recent past issued *catalogues raisonnées* of sections of our collections and others are in preparation (including one on clothing and accessories); we have before published small booklets on the collections, but the Gallery gives an added impetus to this effort. The present booklet on clothing is the first in a new series of such well-illustrated works that will serve the intelligent lay person as an introduction to the subject, as well as a record of what he or she may have seen on a visit to the Wallace Gallery.

This booklet is the work of Linda R. Baumgarten, curator of textiles, who is making an exceptional contribution to the study of this subject. Her distinguished predecessor, Mildred B. Lanier, worked with the collection for many years and helped prepare catalog entries and groups of objects for photography. The beautiful illustrations are the work of the late Delmore Wenzel and the present senior museum photographer, Hans E. Lorenz. Much credit must also go to former chief curators James L. Cogar and John M. Graham III for their important roles in creating and expanding the collection. A publication such as this incorporates many skills, so many of which we are fortunate to find among our colleagues at Colonial Williamsburg, whom we warmly thank.

Graham Hood
Chief Curator

"Dress" or Court Gown and Petticoat. Silk taffeta woven with silver
and decorated with silver lace, bodice and sleeves lined with
linen. England, 1745-1770. 1953-849.

6

Introduction

THE principal focal points of the costume collection at Colonial Williamsburg are more than thirty women's gowns and an equal number of men's suits, all dating between about 1730 and 1800. These are joined by an almost complete range of secondary wearing apparel such as petticoats, breeches, waistcoats, bodices, cloaks, hats, bonnets, shoes, and stockings, as well as accessories including fans, gloves, aprons, stomachers, handkerchiefs, laces, and pocketbooks. A study of such garments makes a contribution to the research on economic and social conditions, as well as adding a colorful and interesting dimension to the story of life in the eighteenth century.

The study of the decorative textiles used in these objects is of major importance to the research being done to establish correct nomenclature and origin of design and manufacture, and it was principally to forward this research that many of these garments were originally acquired. A few random garments were acquired in the early 1930s to serve as basic patterns for the cut of the mid-eighteenth-century reproduction gowns in which a small cadre of hostess-interpreters in the Raleigh Tavern and Governor's Palace were to be dressed. These items were not accessioned until some years later. Nor was a costume collection, as such, envisioned, although many superb eighteenth-century fabrics, made into apparel, had been added to the textile collection in the interim. It was after World War II, at a time when many English

costume collections were being dispersed, and coincidentally at the time the Millinery Shop on Duke of Gloucester Street was being restored, that the substance of the collection was acquired.

The majority of the items acquired at that time came from such prominent collectors and authorities as Dame Doris Langley Moore, founder and patroness of the Museum of Costume in Bath, and the Honorable James Frere, Bluemantle Pursuivant, College of Heralds, whose collection was exhibited for many years at the Victoria and Albert Museum's Lancaster House.

While, regrettably, very few of the costume examples in this collection have a history of ownership in colonial America, it is believed that a parallel may be drawn between these garments and accessories and those mentioned in the rather extensive manuscript holdings of this area — showing how closely dress in colonial Virginia compared with styles fashionable in England during the eighteenth century.

It is notable that the dress of one century often takes on an aura of theatrics when viewed a century or more later, at which time we tend to think of earlier clothing as *costume* and, in so doing, often ascribe to it very dramatic connotations. Appropriate clothing is essential in creating illusions, special effects, or special productions. The characters have been created and must look and react a certain way. To be incorrectly costumed would spoil the illusion. Thus, we often tend to associate the term *costume* with playacting rather than with the apparel of people engaged in daily living. Today, we speak of our wearing apparel as *clothes, styles, fashions;* rarely using the word *costume* to suggest anything other than theatrical or fancy dress. With the thought in mind that we are dealing with people from everyday walks of life, the intention here is to provide the reader with descriptions of the *dress,* or *apparel,* in the eighteenth century, with emphasis on colonial Virginia — making the picture neither more nor less dramatic than the primary source material allows.

Mildred B. Lanier

Acknowledgments

THE author is deeply indebted to Mildred Lanier, who not only acquired many of the garments shown for Williamsburg's collection, but also researched and cataloged them and dressed the mannequins for fully half of the illustrations in this catalog. It was a personal and professional pleasure knowing and working with her. I am also grateful to my other friends and colleagues, both at Colonial Williamsburg and elsewhere, who shared insights, information, research, and their special skills of designing, editing, typing, and photographing. Credit for the beautiful photographs goes to Hans Lorenz and the late Delmore Wenzel.

Linda R. Baumgarten

Purse. Silk and metal threads on silk, France or Germany, 1730-1750. This small purse, measuring 4⅞ inches high, has a central scene that is worked in hundreds of closely spaced French knots. 1985-224.

THE clothing that people wore in the past has the ability to fascinate and involve us as few other objects of their material culture do. Clothing is intimate. Viewing a garment in a museum collection elicits an almost instinctive urge to touch it and try it on ourselves (actions that are, of course, not recommended for reasons of conservation). For some, it is a wish to experience the beautiful fabrics, elaborate decoration, and tactile qualities — experiences no longer found in most of our own clothing. For others, it is a desire to understand people from the past a little better; if we know such details as how they dressed themselves in the morning, what it felt like to be laced into stays, or what it was like to wear coarse linen and woolen while working in a Virginia tobacco field, we might better understand the routine, human aspects of their daily lives, which are so seldom revealed in the written records they left.

The clothing illustrated in this catalog was worn by living people who had much in common with us. Not only did people then respond to fashion, they also varied their garments based on the activity and the formality of the occasion. The eighteenth-century words "dress" and "undress" had meanings quite different from the way we use the words today, though the basic concepts are still viable. "Dress" clothing meant formal clothing with a different set of conventions and accessories from "undress," or informal clothing. In 1775, for example, a woman could still don a pair of exaggerated side hoops, or "panniers," to support her wide skirt for a dress occasion, while her undress clothing — although it would appear quite formal to our eyes — had a more modest skirt size that may not have needed hoops at all. Similarly, the clothes in which a wealthy planter conducted his daily business differed significantly from what he wore to a ball at the Governor's Palace. The garments worn by a blacksmith or dairymaid for daily work were different from their best outfits, reserved for Sundays at church and infrequent special occasions.

Gown. Striped silk taffeta with checked pattern created by extra warp float, bodice and sleeves lined with linen, skirt edges finished with pinking. England or Virginia, 1760-1775. Associated with the Blair family of Virginia. 1983-225.

Textiles and clothing — ephemeral objects that are subject to moth, mildew, and the wear and tear of laundry, restyling, and recycling into quilts or rags — are nevertheless able to help us understand a great deal about history. Consider the fact that a planter's daughter in tidewater Virginia in the 1770s could have worn at the same time a gown of silk from China, underclothing of linen from Holland, and footwear made in England — all shipped in a vast network of trade from their places of origin to a shop or warehouse in London, where they were selected by a merchant, packed for a lengthy voyage across the ocean

Woodcut. This detail illustrated an advertisement for runaway slaves that appeared in the *Virginia Gazette* (Purdie and Dixon), March 28, 1766.

in a ship propelled by wind, to arrive finally in Virginia. Or that a slave — whose very freedom was entangled in a network of trade and commerce — could be wearing clothing made from inexpensive textiles imported especially for his use — a shirt of linen woven in northern Europe, woolen hose from Scotland, or a knitted cap from Monmouth, England. Clothing and accessories worn in eighteenth-century America were selected from sources all over the world.

Some upper-class Virginia men ordered suits custom-made to their measurements in London. They specified expensive fabrics like superfine woolen broadcloth or silks. Their suits were sometimes embellished with imported buttons and other expensive trimmings. Women could also purchase many of their items of apparel, especially petticoats, laces, shoes, stockings, cloaks, aprons, and even stays, ready-made through the import trade. Their gowns were more often made by local seamstresses or mantua makers. Some women made their own clothing, especially work garments and shifts. Only in frontier areas was most clothing homespun and homemade — and even there, traders and storekeepers quickly penetrated the back-country to make imported goods available.

The clothing worn by eighteenth-century Virginians was characterized by great diversity, as one would expect in a society ranging from royal governors and wealthy landowners to indentured servants and slaves. Upper-class Virginians kept abreast of the latest English

Mrs. Thomas Newton, Jr. (Martha Tucker) by John Durand. Oil on canvas. Virginia, ca. 1770. Mrs. Newton of Norfolk, Virginia, wears a sack back gown with self-fabric trimming, sheer neck handkerchief, sleeve ruffles, and a small cap. Gift of M. Knoedler and Company, Inc., G1954-273.

fashions through imported garments, letters from England, news from travelers, and immigrating dressmakers or tailors. Surviving garments, portraits, and written records indicate that when affluent Virginians had occasion to dress up, they were very elegant indeed.

As early as 1724, Hugh Jones wrote in *The Present State of Virginia* that Williamsburg's leading families dressed like the gentry in London. Thirty-five years later, the Reverend Jonathan Boucher described Virginians: "Solomon in all his Glory was not array'd like one of These. I assure you, Mrs. James, the common Planter's Daughters here go every Day in finer Cloaths than I have seen content you for

Sack Back Gown and Matching Petticoat.
Brocaded silk taffeta, linen bodice and sleeve linings, made in England or Virginia, 1760-1770. Worn in Virginia by Elizabeth Dandridge Aylett Henley. Gift of Mrs. R. Keith Kane, G1975-340.

a Summer's Sunday. You thought (homely Creatures as you are) my Sattin Wastecoat was a fine best, Lord help You, I'm noth'g amongst the Lace and Lac'd fellows that are here. Nay, so much does their Taste run after dress that they tell me I may see in Virginia more brilliant Assemblies than I ever c'd in the North of Engl'd, and except Royal Ones P'rhaps in any Part of it."[1]

The concepts of comfort and modesty have always been relative and subject to the influence of fashion and the needs of the occasion. Like us, eighteenth-century people needed clothing for warmth and comfort, but they quickly abandoned those needs if fashion or

Mrs. Gavin Lawson (Susannah Rose) by John Hesselius. Oil on canvas. Virginia, dated 1770. Mrs. Lawson, the wife of a planter and merchant of Stafford County, Virginia, wears a satin gown with stomacher front, fine lace, and pearls. 1954-262.

the occasion dictated. During much of the eighteenth century, women's skirts were long and the sleeves covered the elbows; yet a woman would readily push up her sleeves and hike up her petticoats while doing laundry or working in the dairy, and, when fashion dictated it, women would shorten their skirts to the ankles, as many did in the 1780s.

When we look at ladies' corsets — "stays" — from the period, we cannot imagine how a woman could subject herself to such a garment. Yet the wearing of stays was as much linked to concepts of modesty and support as it was to figure shape; without her stays for most public occasions, a woman was considered not quite properly dressed at best and a "loose woman" at worst. Someone who had worn stays from girlhood might scarcely have questioned their comfort or lack of it. (And

who is to say that stays were any more uncomfortable than pointed-toe, high-heeled twentieth-century shoes?)

Climate also had a significant effect on clothing. In the sultry climate of Virginia many, even the upper classes, chose washable linen or cotton clothing for informal wear. A traveler in the early 1730s described the summer clothing of Virginians: "In Summertime even the gentry goe Many in White Holland [linen] Wast Coat and drawers and a thin Cap on their heads and Thread stockings [knitted linen]. The Ladyes Strait laced in thin Silk or Linnen. In Winter [they dress] mostly as in England and affect London Dress and wayes."[2]

During the hot summer months, men often wore unlined coats and thin waistcoats of cotton or linen fabrics. Advising his brother

Summer Coat and Breeches. Coarse homespun cotton, unlined, Isle of Wight County or Goochland County, Virginia, 1780-1790. The suit is sized to fit a youth (the breeches have a 27-inch waist). 1964-174.

about what to wear when he attended the College of William and Mary, Stephen Hawtrey wrote, "Your Coathing in summer must be as thin and light as possible for the heat is beyond your conception . . . your Cloth suit unlined may do for the Month of May, but after that time you must wear the thinnest Stuffs that can be made without lining [;] some people . . . wear brown holland [linen] Coats with lining — some Crape — You must carry with you a Stock of Linnen Waistcoats made very large and loose, that they may'nt stick to your hide when you perspire."[3]

Many Virginia women favored gowns made of lustring, a crisp, light silk that was often ordered for wear during the summer months. When the hot weather became unbearable, some women went without their stays for informal occasions and at home, although formal occasions still required them. One Virginia woman related in her diary that she did not bother to get dressed immediately on a particularly "sulterry" day; she remained "up stairs in only shift and petticoat till after Tea."[4]

Clothing that reaches a museum collection has been culled by time, by curatorial selectivity, and by a process we might call "the survival of the finest." Most collections contain garments that are of the elegant, dress type, simply because everyday clothing has not survived. No one thought to save the plain, worn garments of a lower-class man or woman — if there was anything left to save but rags. To understand what most people wore in the past, museum collections need to be supplemented by carefully analyzed print sources and written records.

Some questions about people's appearance cannot be answered to our satisfaction, even after poring over all the surviving sources. We would very much like to know the size of the "average" person in the eighteenth century, but we can offer only partial answers. We do know that the unaltered bodices and stays in Williamsburg's collections have waistlines

Gown and Matching Petticoat. Cream silk taffeta with crisp finish — "lustring" — trimmed with pinked self-fabric, linen bodice and sleeve linings. By tradition made in England in 1778 and brought to Virginia by Mrs. Frances Norton. Gift of Mr. George Baylor, G1946-133.

ranging from 21½ inches to 34 inches, with an average of slightly over 25 inches. Two hundred and twenty-five men advertised as being runaways in the *Virginia Gazette* between the years 1750 to 1770 had an average height of 5 feet, 7½ inches. Based on limited, non-scientific samples, these figures cannot be taken as averages for an entire period. Research continues in all aspects of appearance and clothing.

Wooden Doll with Clothing Showing Typical Layering of Women's Underwear. The 23½-inch-tall doll wears a linen shift, boned stays, two cotton underpetticoats pleated to narrow tape waistbands, a pocket, a silk satin petticoat, and a sack back silk gown with a stomacher front and skirt drawn up in "polonaise" fashion, France, 1770s. 1966-169, 1966-170.

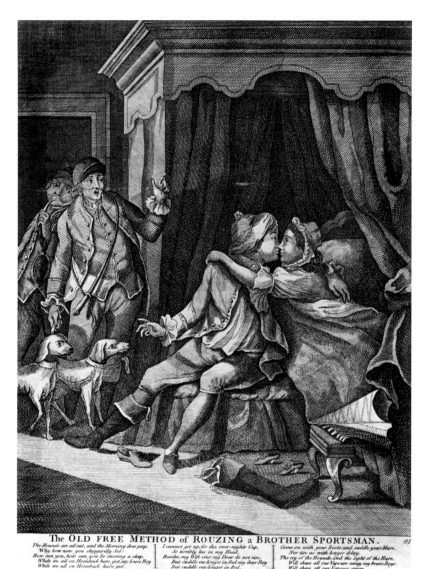

The OLD FREE METHOD of ROUZING a BROTHER SPORTSMAN. *81*

***The Old Free Method of Rouzing
a Brother Sportsman.*** Line engraving. Printed for Carington
Bowles, London, 1755-1760.
The woman wears a shift and
cap; her stays lie on the chair.
1967-327.

WOMEN generally wore more layers of underwear in the eighteenth century than is customary today. A loose fitting white linen or cotton shift that had sleeves to the elbows and came to just below the knees was the undermost garment. (Most English and American women did not wear underdrawers or pantalets until the nineteenth century.) Because a shift was worn at all times beneath a woman's outer clothing, it helped prevent body oils and perspiration from soiling and staining the garments. Shifts were also worn as sleepwear. Although a wealthy woman might own enough clothing so that she had shifts specifically for sleeping, a poor woman slept in the same shift she wore under her clothes in the daytime. In the eighteenth century, "nightgown" usually referred to a type of informal dress and not to a sleeping garment.

Shifts were cut along straight lines directly on the fabric in a series of rectangles and triangles to avoid wasting more than a few inches of material. Triangular gores in the skirt gave it extra fullness; gussets under the arms achieved their shaping. Surviving Virginia accounts indicate that shifts required around 3¼ to 3½ yards of linen, which typically ranged in width from "three-quarters wide" (27 inches) to "yard wide" (36 inches). A larger woman cut her shift out of wider linen. Shifts were sewn with careful, close stitches that would not pull out under stress since they were subjected to vigorous laundering.

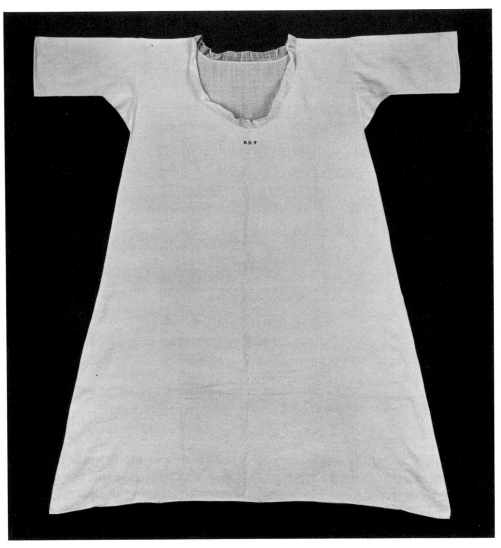

Shift Worn under Women's Clothing. White linen, woven lace at the neckline, Europe, late eighteenth or early nineteenth century. The initials R. D. P. are worked in silk cross stitches at the neckline. 1983-234.

Tight Lacing, or Fashion before Ease. Hand-colored mezzotint. Bowles and Carver after John Collet, England, 1770-1775. 1969-111.

Ladies' Undergarments. Shift, white linen, Europe, eighteenth century. Boned stays, linen, England, 1740-1760. Petticoat, cotton and linen dimity worked with crewel wools, New England, 1745-1760. 1984-79, 1935-96, 1956-578.

A woman laced her stays, a corset stiffened with whalebone, packthread, wood, or metal, onto her upper body over her shift. Stays had an important influence on the posture and body shape of eighteenth-century women. Laced with cords through eyelets at the back or front, stays shaped the upper body into a cone, held the shoulders back and created a narrow-shouldered appearance, and helped maintain erect posture. They rose from the waist up to the center of the bustline, and because they did not have cups to accommodate the bosom, they pushed the fullness of the bust into a high, rounded shape.

Although stays were sometimes tightly laced for fashionable wear, a practice that was widely satirized in prints, they did not necessarily restrict movement drastically or result in unusually small waistlines except among those who carried the fashion to extreme. That all women in the eighteenth century did not have

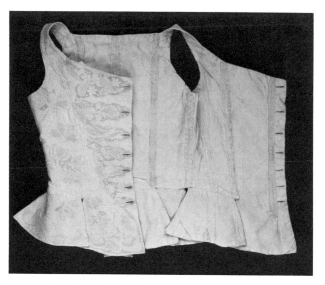

Bodice. Possibly called a waistcoat or jumps. Fine white cotton, cord quilted and worked with French knots, linen lining with widely spaced tapes enclosing bones, Europe, first half of eighteenth century. Eyelets at armholes indicate that the garment once had tie-in sleeves. It has been slightly altered at the waistline. Anonymous gift, G1971-1566.

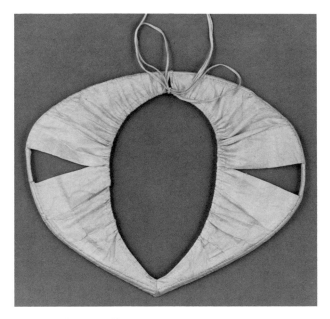

Hoops. Linen stiffened with whalebone. Belonging to the gown on page 28, the hoops were worn around the waist under the gown petticoat to hold the skirts out, with side slits for access to pockets. England, 1770s. 1968-646.

small waistlines is borne out in the collections surviving at Williamsburg: several gowns have waists from twenty-seven up to thirty inches, and one pair of stays has a waistline of thirty-four inches!

Many working women wore stays as support garments, though their stays were not laced as tightly or boned as heavily as those worn for dress occasions. Mrs. Scott, a member of Virginia Governor Dunmore's household, sent an order for stays to London among the other goods ordered by the governor. She did not want her stays to be made too restrictive: "I dont mind the fashion if they are made easy and full in the Stomick."[5]

Women sometimes wore lighter support garments, called "jumps," in place of stays. Unboned or partially boned bodices, jumps were worn informally at home or whenever a less stiff garment was required.

Women wore one or more underpetticoats,

which resembled full skirts. When her gown required hoops to hold out the fullness of the skirt, a woman fastened them around her waist or wore a petticoat with hoops built in. Since gowns did not have pockets, a woman might tie one or a pair of separate pockets around her waist. The pockets were reached through slits left open in the skirts of the upper petticoat and the gown. If the gown had an open skirt, the upper petticoat would be of a fabric that harmonized with the gown and was intended to be seen. Thus the word "petticoat," often shortened to "coat," did not necessarily mean only an undergarment.

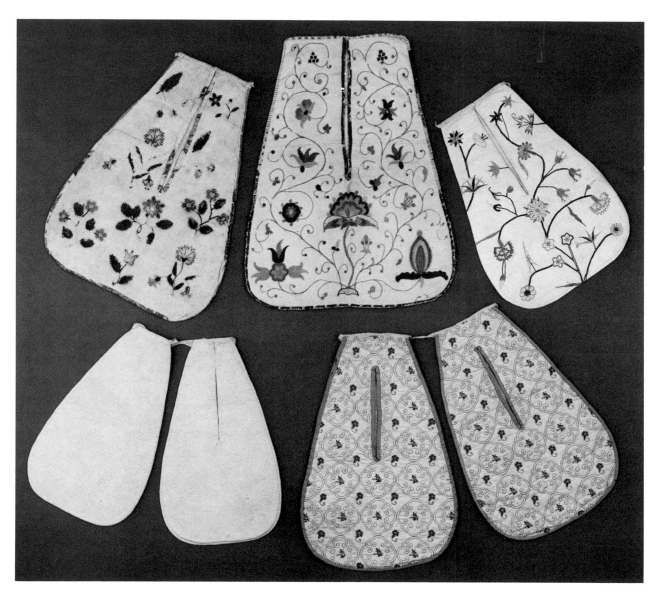

Tie-on Pockets. Clockwise from upper left: crewel wool needlework on cotton and linen, New England, 1765-1775; crewel wool needlework on cotton and linen, New England, 1740-1770; silk needlework on linen, probably Europe, 1775-1800; silk needlework on linen, England, 1740-1760; white cord quilted cotton, Europe, 1700-1750. G1974-264, 1963-11, 1958-409, 1956-302, 1-2, and G1971-1584, 1-2.

LADIES' gowns were often made with the skirts open at the front to reveal a matching or contrasting petticoat, and the bodice was shaped to be worn with a separate decorative triangular-shaped insert called a stomacher, which was pinned or laced in place. By selecting different petticoats and stomachers, a lady could alter the appearance of her ensemble without adding to her wardrobe. The idea of mixing and matching one's clothing is certainly not new.

The gowns illustrated have wide skirts that were held out by hoops constructed of cane, wire, or whalebone held together by tapes or sewn into a petticoat. The size and shape of hoops varied during the century as fashion dictated; ladies' skirts took on their most exaggerated width in the middle of the eighteenth century, then gradually decreased during the 1760s. Wearing wide hoops required careful thought before a woman entered a doorway or carriage or sat down. Because of their inhibiting effects, they were usually reserved for dress or formal occasions. Wide hoop skirts continued to be worn at court into the nineteenth century, although by then they were considered to be outdated for daily wear.

Gown, Stomacher, Petticoat, and Sleeve Ruffles. Gown, pink ribbed silk (faded to beige) brocaded with multicolor flowers, bodice and sleeves lined with linen. England, 1745-1750. Stomacher, linen embroidered and quilted with back stitches in silk, England, 1725-1750. Petticoat, pale green silk satin quilted in running stitches to glazed worsted back, woolen batting, England, 1750-1775. Sleeve ruffles, sheer cotton worked with satin stitches and open work, England, 1750-1765. 1947-506, 1953-314, 1941-211, 2, 1953-860.

Gown, Stomacher, and Petticoat. Gown, cream silk taffeta brocaded with multicolor flowers (relined and altered at the waistline), England, 1745-1755. Stomacher, silk with silk and metallic needlework, probably England, 1730-1750. Petticoat, dark green silk satin quilted in running stitches to glazed worsted back, woolen batting, England, 1750-1770. 1953-854, 1955-373, 1953-851.

Sack Back Gown (shown from back). Coral pink striped silk brocaded with flowers, bodice and sleeves lined with linen, England, 1760-1770. 1953-848.

THE backs of women's gowns were usually styled in one of two graceful fashions. Sometimes the fabric was designed to fall loosely in deep pleats from the back shoulders; this was called a "sack back" or "robe à la Française." The fashion survived with various modifications until the last quarter of the eighteenth century. The other style had the pleats sewn down close to the back; it was the "robe à l'Anglaise," sometimes also called a "nightgown."

The two dresses shown here are made of brocaded and damask-woven silks, which were very popular choices for fashionable women's wear. These types of silk fabrics were woven in narrow widths (the silks illustrated measure 19¾ inches and 22 inches wide), so a gown with a matching petticoat might require as much as twenty yards or more. A similar style made of wider printed cotton required less fabric.

The sleeves end in the graceful flounces over the elbow that were at the height of fashion during the 1760s and early 1770s. The direction of the stripe in the brocaded gown indicates that the sleeves were cut crosswise on the fabric so the stripes ran around the arm, not lengthwise. This method of cutting sleeves was not at all unusual for even the most elegant garments.

Gown or Robe à l'Anglaise (shown from back). Light blue green silk damask, linen bodice and sleeve linings, England, 1760-1770. 1960-714.

Gown and Petticoat. Gown, cream silk brocaded with flowers, linen bodice and sleeve linings, England, 1720s, altered to the style of the 1770s. The unlined skirt of this gown is finished with pinked scallops worked with an iron tool. Petticoat, pale yellow silk tabby weave quilted with back stitches to a worsted wool twill backing with woolen batting (see detail). The petticoat is signed and dated in the quilting "Abigail Trowbridge, 1750," By tradition worn in Connecticut; made in Connecticut or England. 1951-150, 1952-19.

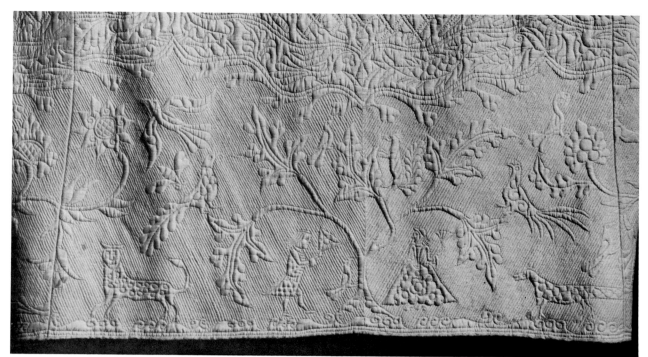

Petticoat (detail). The petticoat has marvelous human figures, animals, and plants quilted around its lower border. The front of the petticoat has the British coat of arms. 1952-19.

SOME gowns, styled to be worn without stomachers, closed at the center front of the bodice with pins or hooks and eyes. The two gowns illustrated on pages 24 and 26 have numerous small holes indicating that they were pinned together.

Silk gowns were frequently trimmed or finished with decorative pinking, a serrated edge created by means of a sharp tool that cut through folded layers of fabric when struck with a mallet or hammer. Pinked edges on crisp, closely woven silks did not require any other finish, and most have not raveled significantly in over two hundred years.

Quilted petticoats, sometimes called "quilted coats" or "wearing quilts," were fashionable for wear with open robes. Since they were constructed of layers, usually with a woolen batting between, quilted petticoats helped keep the wearer warm in an era before central heating.

Pinking Tool. Iron/steel, probably eighteenth century. Shown with reproduction silk fabric pinked with the tool. Anonymous gift, G1971-2049.

Gown, Petticoat, and Neck Handkerchief (and detail). Gown, brown ribbed
silk, linen bodice and sleeve linings, attributed to Pennsylvania, 1760-1780.
Its color and size (waist 30 inches) suggest that it was worn by a mature
woman. Petticoat, cream silk satin quilted in running stitches to glazed
worsted backing, woolen batting, England, 1760-1775. Neck handkerchief,
white cotton in a triangular shape, hemmed on three sides, Delaware or
Pennsylvania, 1780-1810. 1983-227, 1960-731, G1983-303, gift of Frances Matthews.

Petticoat. Blue green silk satin quilted with running stitches to linen back, cotton batting, 1770-1775. (Waistband and hem binding missing.) By family tradition ordered from London by Mrs. Gabriel Galt (Elizabeth Ege). The linen backing and cotton filling suggest that the petticoat might have been made in Virginia rather than England. 1978-76.

WEAVERS and dressmakers produced incomparable examples of what can only be called art. The sack back gown shown is made of crisp ivory silk, heavily brocaded with silver gilt in a lively, undulating pattern of leaves and exotic flowers. Gathered ruching down the front of the skirt echoes the pattern on the silk itself. The stomacher is fashioned of silver gilt lace and sequins. Oval hoops tied around the waist hold the skirt out with modest fullness at the sides (see illustration on page 18). Only the very wealthy could afford an elaborate gown such as this, which was worn for formal full dress occasions.

Although the history of this garment is unknown, much can be inferred from the evidence of its construction. It has areas of old stitching, piecing, and folds, showing that it was remade from an existing gown, which was not unusual, even at the high social level this garment indicates. The practice was universal among less wealthy people who had to make their clothing last for years. Expensive fabrics were not allowed to lie unworn just because a garment had gone out of style or the wearer had changed size. This fact of eighteenth-century life makes it all the more difficult for museums today to find unaltered clothing, especially that worn by the middle and lower classes.

Sack Back Gown (front and back). Silk taffeta brocaded in metallic silver gilt, England, silks probably Spitalfields, ca. 1750. The gown was altered at a later date, probably the 1770s. 1968-646.

Stomacher. Silver gilt lace, paper, floss silk, England, 1770s. 1968-646.

WHILE some of the most opulent and elegant clothing imaginable was produced in the eighteenth century, most men and women worked long hours for a living at physically demanding tasks, and their clothing was adapted to accommodate their less glamorous — even tedious — lives. Working women often shortened their skirts to the ankle or above so they would not trip or catch fire while cooking over an open hearth. They sometimes tucked their skirts up in their waistbands to get them out of the way. When they wore stays for working, as many women did, they laced themselves less tightly, enabling them to bend and stretch, or they wore less heavily boned stays. In place of fashionable gowns with tight bodices, long skirts, and wide hoops, working women usually wore short, loose garments, variously called "short gowns" or "bed gowns." These garments were made with sleeves cut full and straight to allow

La Pharmacie Rustique (detail). Line and stipple engraving. Engraved by Barthelemi Hubner, France, 1775. Although the engraver has included some symbolic elements, the garments the woman wears — a jacket laced over a neck handkerchief, shortened petticoat, and shoes with practical low heels — are typical of those worn while working and for informal occasions. 1959-437.

ease of movement. Because they were not closely fitted, they were also practical during pregnancy.[6]

Another type of working garment was a more fitted sleeved jacket or waistcoat that appears to have fastened by lacing through eyelets up the front, or with buttons. Such bodices and petticoats formed a kind of two-piece working suit for many slave women in Virginia. Venus, a seventeen-year-old slave, ran away wearing a petticoat and waistcoat of green plains, an inexpensive woolen fabric. Her waistcoat was described as being somewhat different from the usual, having "metal buttons and button holes instead of a lace before, and without skirts."[7] This description suggests that her waistcoat ended at the waist, without the peplum effect formed by tabs extending below. Female slaves on Robert Carter's plantation were provided with a jacket, petticoat, and two shifts each; apparently no stays were issued. It seems possible that two

Woman's Short Unfitted Gown. Block-printed cotton, England, 1775-1800. This style of loose working garment was probably called a "bedgown." 1985-242.

shifts were given to each woman so one could be laundered while the other was being worn.

Middle-class women's gowns were not made of the best silks, though a woman might own one gown of less expensive silk for best wear; everyday dresses were linen, often striped "holland" or worsted mixtures such as "camblet." Many lower- and middle-class free women owned warm petticoats quilted of wool fabrics.

The clothing of the lower classes in Virginia may not have been as elegant or refined as that of the gentry, but it was often colorful. Consider the servant woman who ran away attired in "fine Pink coloured Worsted Stockings" along with a brown quilted petticoat, a checked apron, and a striped bed gown, or another who was wearing a black hat, "an old red Silk Handkerchief round her Neck, an old dirty blue Stuff Gown, with check Linen Cuffs, old Stays, a black and white strip'd Country Cloth Petticoat, an old blue quilted ditto, a check Linen Apron and a brown Linen Shift" [probably unbleached linen].[8]

The Elopement (detail) by John Collet. Oil on canvas. England, 1755-1765. The woman wears a loose shortened gown, probably called a bedgown, over a patched petticoat. 1969-48, 2.

THE attitudes and clothing of the working classes were not without their influence in the late eighteenth century. The period from the late 1760s through the end of the century was one of worldwide activity in fashion as well as politics. The crisis that resulted in the American Revolution spurred colonists on to produce their own fabrics and clothing. At a ball in Williamsburg in 1769 it was observed that the ladies, "to the number of near one hundred, appeared in homespun gowns."[9] This effort was short lived, however, and after hostilities ended, trade in imported goods soon resumed.

More importantly, both the American Revolution and the French Revolution may be seen in part as dramatic episodes in a process that had begun some years before: the rise of the common man and woman who, for a variety of interconnecting reasons, came in the late eighteenth century to have more of society's goods available to them than ever before. This development has been called the Consumer Revolution, and even fashion was commercialized and democratized.[10] It is instructive that the frock coat and long trousers of the workingman evolved into high fashion by the end of this period.

Not only were more people from the middle and lower classes able to afford more and more fashionable clothing — the lady's maid was often observed to be as well dressed as the lady herself — but the fashions changed more rapidly. Better means of communication spread news of the changes more quickly.

Ladies' fashion magazines, inexpensive cardboard fashion dolls with a variety of cut-out clothing, and more advertising helped to increase the pace of change.

Silhouette and cut of clothing changed more rapidly than ever before. The last quarter of the century saw the fashionable ascent of less formal styles, some borrowed from the working classes, polonaise gowns with their skirts puffed up like the tucked skirts of the dairymaid, bustle effects, the lengthening of sleeves over the elbow, elaborate hair styles and hats, and, finally, the tubular silhouette inspired by the classical drapery of Greek statues.

Paper Doll. Watercolor on paper, England, 1780-1790. This hand-painted paper doll, part of a family of four, is inscribed on the back "Sally Guzzle wife to Mr. Sampson Guzzle in her youth Esteem'd Pretty." Probably made as a satirical toy and not as a fashion doll, Mrs. Guzzle nevertheless wears the fashionable clothing and accessories of the 1780s and might have served to transmit fashion information to some extent. 1969-129.

Fitted Bodice and Petticoat (shown from back). The upper garment, probably called a jacket, is of block-printed cotton lined with linen, with eyelets at the front for lacing close to the torso, probably France, 1775-1785. Although jackets were often worn by working-class women, the relatively expensive printed fabric in this example suggests that it may have been the everyday or informal wear of a middle-class woman rather than a laborer. Petticoat, blue green ribbed silk quilted in running stitches to blue worsted backing, woolen batting, probably England, 1760-1775. 1962-259, G1974-269, bequest of Grace H. Westerfield.

Jacket, Petticoat, Neck Handkerchief, and Sleeve Ruffles. Jacket, Indian mordant-painted and dyed cotton chintz, lined with cotton and linen, France, 1770-1785. The jacket, possibly called a "caraco" during the period, has a fitted back and shortened skirt. The mock stomacher is actually sewn to the bodice and closes at center front, with a flap for holding a neck handkerchief in place. Petticoat, rose worsted quilted with running stitches to worsted back, woolen batting, England, 1755-1775. Neck handkerchief, sheer white cotton with white needlework, Europe, 1770-1780. Sleeve ruffles, cotton with subtle woven check pattern created by crossed heavier threads, Europe, 1750-1775. 1953-736, 1955-241, 1953-858, 1954-67.

The SPRUCE SPORTSMAN, or BEAUTY the BEST SHOT.

Printed for & Sold by CARINGTON BOWLES, at his Map & Print Warehouse, N.º69 in St Pauls Church Yard, LONDON. Publish'd as the Act directs, 24 June 1780.

The Spruce Sportsman, or Beauty the Best Shot. Hand-colored mezzotint engraving. Printed by Carington Bowles, London, 1780. The ladies wear the tall hair styles and hats of the 1770s and 1780s — perhaps somewhat exaggerated by the engraver. The large black hat is the caned, collapsible form known as a calash. The servant woman, although dressed more modestly, wears a fashionably large cap. 1958-356.

DURING the 1770s and 1780s it became fashionable to loop the skirt up in puffs "à la Polonaise" either by pulling the ends through the pocket slits in the skirt or by using sewn-in tapes. At the same time the pleats in the skirt became smaller. This fashion required light, crisp fabrics to achieve the desired effect — fabrics such as lustring, a silk specially treated to give it a crisp texture. The bodice detail illustrates one method for drawing the skirt in polonaise style, that is, by using sewn-in tapes intended to be tied together. Also apparent in the detail is the absence of bustline darts on an unaltered eighteenth-century bodice due to the body-shaping effect of the stays worn beneath it.

Polonaise Gown and Petticoat (and detail). Gown, pale lavender silk taffeta lustring now faded to pink, bodice and sleeves lined with white linen, England, 1770-1780. The skirt is drawn up in the "polonaise" style by means of narrow tapes sewn about 22 inches apart on the inside and designed to be tied together (see detail). Petticoat, pink silk satin quilted with running stitches to white glazed worsted backing, woolen batting dyed pink, England, 1760-1775. 1983-233, 1953-436.

Polonaise Gown and Matching Petticoat. Cream silk taffeta lustring trimmed with silk gauze, bodice lined with linen, sleeves restored and relined, England, 1775-1785. The skirt is drawn up by means of cords that run through thread loops sewn to the inside of the skirt. 1960-719.

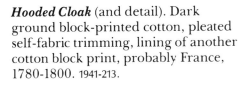

Woman's Hooded Cloak. Red wool broadcloth, modern lining, England, 1750-1810. 1953-968.

Hooded Cloak (and detail). Dark ground block-printed cotton, pleated self-fabric trimming, lining of another cotton block print, probably France, 1780-1800. 1941-213.

IN cold weather, women wore full capes, called cloaks, of varying lengths that frequently had a hood to pull up over the head. Cloaks went by many names, depending on their exact style — cardinal, rocket, tippet, shade, capuchin, pelisse, pelerine — and were made in a variety of fabrics. The red wool broadcloth cloak was one of the most popular for outdoor wear in rural areas of England and the colonies. Philip Vickers Fithian described Virginia ladies in December 1773: "Almost every Lady wears a red Cloak; and when they ride out they tye a white handkerchief over their Head and face, so that when I first came into Virginia, I was distress'd whenever I saw a Lady, for I thought She had the Tooth-Ach!"[11] Fithian was describing large square or triangular kerchiefs known as handkerchiefs in the eighteenth century. They were usually worn about the neck and shoulders for modesty and warmth with low-cut gowns, although sometimes women tied this handkerchief about their heads like a scarf. The neck handkerchief was called a fichu in the nineteenth century.

Women also wore gloves and muffs, and they added extra petticoats and underwaistcoats in cold weather. Late in the century the long greatcoat came into fashion, but it did not replace the hooded cloak entirely.

March. Hand-colored mezzotint engraving. Printed for Robert Sayer, England, 1767. The young woman wears a short hooded cloak and carries a fur muff; her straw hat, worn over a cap, has the typical wide brim and flat crown fashionable in the 1750s and 1760s. 1941-239.

WOMEN could choose from a variety of accessories to complement their clothing. Headwear formed an important part of a lady's wardrobe, since it was customary for a grown woman to wear a cap at all times when not actually in formal clothing. For formal occasions, she often dressed her hair with ribbons, pearls, or artificial flowers (see page 11). Hats varied greatly in shape and material. One of the most enduring styles was a flat straw or silk covered hat with a shallow crown. When hair styles took on extra height in the 1770s and 1780s, women wore a calash, a collapsible affair of silk and cane that stood above the tall hair style without crushing it.

Many of a lady's accessories could be purchased from a female milliner, who not only made headwear but also acted as a retailer for a variety of imported fabrics and fashion accessories.

The Studious Fair. Hand-colored mezzotint engraving. Printed by Henry Parker and Robert Sayer, England, 1760. The woman wears a shaped cap, elaborate sleeve ruffles, and a sheer apron with sack back gown; on her wrist is a miniature portrait worn as a bracelet. 1971-477.

Two Laces. Cap lappet (streamer hanging down from cap) and edging for a lady's gown or man's shirt, linen bobbin lace, Flanders, 1720-1750. 1953-177, 1953-153.

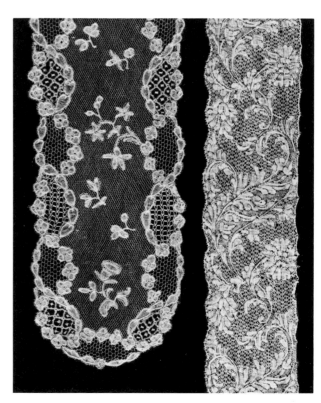

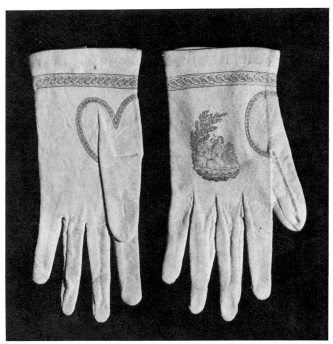

Woman's Gloves (and detail). Printed chamois leather, England, 1791. The words "F. Bull & Co. Jan 4th, 1791" are printed beneath the thumbs of these gloves. 1985-218, 1-2.

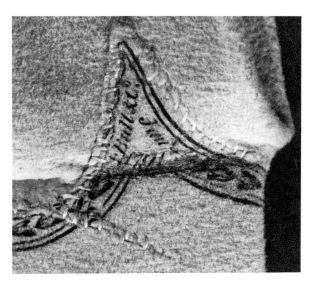

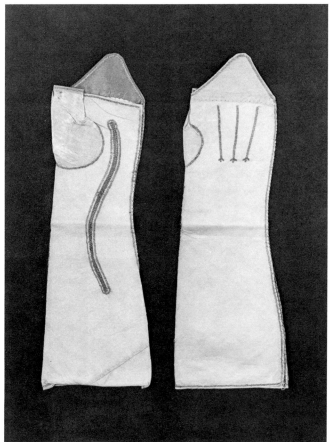

Mitts. Embroidered silk with leather lining, England, 1760-1780. Intended to be worn with women's elbow-length gowns, mitts were worn with the points folded back over the hand, leaving the fingers free for handwork. 1985-216, 1-2.

Women's Accessories. Calash bonnet, green silk taffeta lined with pink silk, probably England, 1770-1790. Hat, straw covered with cream silk, gauze trimming, England, 1760-1780. Fan, oriental export, painted and silvered paper leaf, bamboo sticks, carried in 1770 by Anna Clifford of Philadelphia, gift of Miss Beatrix Rumford. Neck handkerchief, cotton with silk chain stitch needlework, England, 1780-1800. Muff, cream silk satin embroidered with silk, probably England, 1780-1790, gift of Mrs. Thomas L. Wattles. Pocketbook, blue silk taffeta with pink silk chain stitch needlework stating "Tout est Plaisir/Quand on Aime" (All is pleasure when one loves), France,

1780-1800. Carnation, paper and wire, possibly eighteenth century. Miniature book, *The Bible in Miniature Or a Concise History of the Old & New Testament in Verse,* Coventry, Luckman & Suffield, n.d. but probably mid-eighteenth century. Handbag, pink silk taffeta with silk needlework, bobbin lace, and silk flowers, France, 1775-1800. Miniature painting, William Fauquier by "J. S." (probably John Smart), framed to be worn as a bracelet, England, 1761, gift of Mr. Gilbert Fauquier. Miniature portrait of an unknown man, framed with a loop to be worn on a ribbon around the neck, England, 1760-1775. 1960-723, 1970-104, G1980-238, 1, 1951-273, G1954-18, G1971-1400, 1952-512, 1947-552, 1958-26, G1973-246, 1979-58.

APRONS of washable fabrics were
functional garments, indispens-
able for protecting clothing while
working or caring for children.
Other aprons in the eighteenth century were
made of beautifully embroidered and lace-
trimmed fabrics to be worn as fashion accessories. Aprons usually tied about the waist with
narrow tapes, or "apron strings." Sometimes
dress aprons had matching sleeve ruffles and
neck handkerchiefs.

Apron. Block-printed cotton, France,
1770-1780. The bib was designed to be
pinned to the bodice. In the nineteenth
century, this "pinner" form evolved into
the pinafore. Shown with a silk gown of
the 1770s. 1952-67, 1947-509.

Apron. Sheer white linen worked with fine
chain stitches and drawn work, England or
Continental Europe, 1770-1790. Anonymous gift, G1971-1547.

Hand Screen or Fan. "Keep Within Compass." Painted line engraving on paper backed with painted silk, England, 1785-1795. 1950-379.

May. Hand-colored mezzotint engraving, transferred to glass. Published by T. Burford, England, 1745-1747. Among the accessories worn and carried by the young woman are a fan, a lappet cap, pearls, and a watch hanging from her waist. 1967-460, 5.

DURING the eighteenth century, fans were far more important as a fashion accessory than for cooling one's self on hot days. Special fans were made with decorations appropriate for carrying while attending religious services or in mourning. Along with more frivolous fans decorated with amorous scenes or instructions for playing card games, some fans, like the printed example illustrated, had moralistic messages, admonishing their owners to "Keep Within Compass," or to "Fear God, Know Thyself, Bridle thy Will, and Remember thy End."

The use of the fan for flirtation was sati-rized as early as 1711 when Joseph Addison wrote in the London *Spectator* that "women are armed with Fans as Men with Swords, and sometimes do more Execution with them."[12] The "language of the fan" — using various movements of the fan to convey specific mean-ings — appears to have developed in Spain, and was translated and republished in English during the nineteenth century. Although there is no evidence that colonial women used their fans to communicate via a special lan-guage of the fan, they may well have flirted with them during social occasions. The sub-tleties of body language have always been with us.

Fan. Ivory inlaid with mother of pearl and brass, paper leaf printed and painted with a scene from the 1739 Battle of Portobello, England, 1740. See page 66 for a detail. 1981-195.

Ladies' Shoes. Back to front: brocaded silk with applied silver trim, 1720-1740; clog, brocaded silk and leather with metallic trim, 1720-1740; green satin trimmed with narrow green braid, 1720-1745; green worsted damask, 1730-1750; blue silk satin with silver lace, 1730-1750; mule, brocaded silk with leather heel, 1750-1760; brocaded silk, labeled by John Hose, London, 1750-1765; green silk satin, labeled by Gresham's, London, marked in ink, "Small 6," 1770-1780; cream silk satin with ribbon bow, 1780-1795; blue silk taffeta, ca. 1800. 1954-1024, 1954-1026, 1954-1025, 1964-476, 1954-905, 1953-983, 1953-106, 1957-148, 1964-393, 1977-265.

SHOES underwent several stylistic evolutions during the century. Frequently, especially very early and again late in the century, they tied over the instep. At other times they were fastened with buckles, which were interchangeable and, being made of silver, brass, sparkling paste stones, or even jewels, were often highly decorative and expensive. Working-class men and women wore inexpensive metal buckles or shoes that fastened by tying. Late in the century, slip-on shoes for women became fashionable.

Women's shoes were made of elegant but fragile fabrics such as silk and worsted, as well as of more functional leather; men's shoes and boots were leather. Shoes were made on a straight last, meaning there was no distinction between right and left feet.

Although shoemakers and bootmakers made footwear to order and ready-made imported shoes were available in colonial stores, some upper-class colonists ordered shoes for themselves and their servants directly from England. One wonders how well such shoes fit when they arrived, since they were often ordered by length in inches or even by a child's age! Virginian William Nelson ordered shoes for one of his boys, "8 pr of strong Shoes and Pumps for a Boy of eight years old."[13]

Sometimes shoes were designated by size, although the use of standard sizes was by no means universal. The orders of Virginia planter Robert Carter indicate that his wife's shoes were "small fives." A pair of dark green satin shoes in Williamsburg's collection are marked in ink in the lining, "small 6"; these shoes correspond in length to a modern woman's size 6.

Shoe (one of a pair). Leather with linen lining and silk tie, England, ca. 1790. The shoe is labeled "MARTIN and M'MILLAN Ladies Shoe Warehouse, No. 111, Jermain-st, St. James's, From Mr. Hogg's, (Late Messrs. Hogg and Brown's[)]." 1985-238, 1.

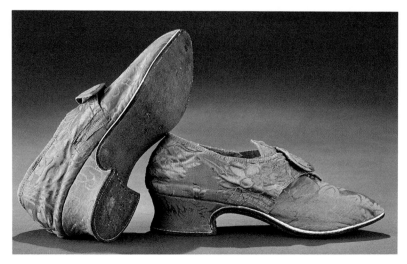

Shoes. Silk damask with linen and leather linings, probably England, 1740-1760. 1985-236, 1-2.

STOCKINGS were knitted of wool, linen (also called thread), cotton, or silk in a variety of colors. White silk stockings were most frequently worn for formal occasions. Although some stockings were knitted by hand on needles, many were knitted in flat pieces to the desired shape on machines called stocking frames, and then were seamed up the back. The clocks — ornamental designs at the ankles — were embroidered or knitted in.

Working-class people, Indians, slaves, and laborers wore either coarsely knitted stockings or stockings made of inexpensive wool fabrics cut and sewn to fit the contours of the leg, more or less.

Stockings were held up by ribbon-like garters tied above the knee. Men often fastened the breeches band tightly just below their knees to keep their stockings in place.

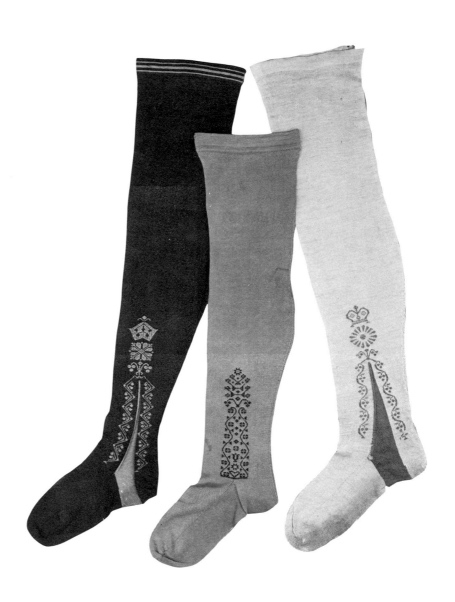

Women's or Men's Stockings *(see page 79)*. Left to right: dark green knitted silk, probably England, ca. 1750; pink knitted silk, England or Continental Europe, ca. 1750; cream knitted linen thread with silk design at clocks, probably England, first half of the eighteenth century. 1954-1051, X1975-182, 1967-131.

IN informal situations, men often wore long, loose gowns called "banyans" instead of a coat. Light gowns were especially useful in the hot climate of the South. Philip Vickers Fithian, tutor to Robert Carter's children at Nomini Hall plantation, wrote of the Virginia heat in his diary entry of July 29, 1774: "I dress in a thin waist-Coat, [and] a loose, light linen Gown; The Boys, Harry and Bob have nothing on, in School, but their shirts and Breeches."[14]

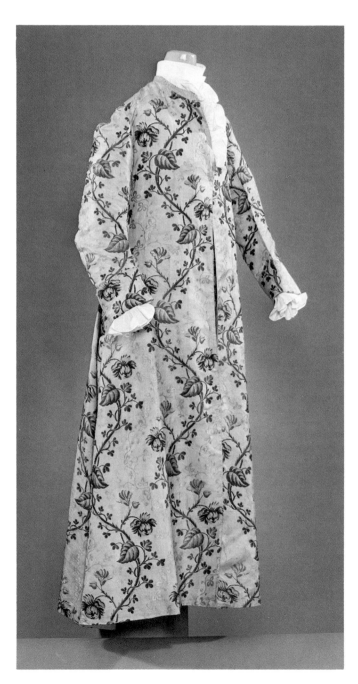

Man's Gown or "Banyan." Floral patterned brocaded silk lined with white linen and cotton mixture, fabric, probably England, ca. 1750; gown remade 1760-1775. Alterations from an earlier garment are in evidence. 1941-208.

M EN'S underwear was far less elaborate than women's. Some men wore linen or cotton under-drawers as liners for their breeches, though few samples have survived to show exactly how they looked.

Sometimes worn without a coat or waistcoat during vigorous work or at home, men's shirts served as both underwear and outerwear. Like women's shifts, shirts were usually cut from a full width of linen in a series of rectangles and squares without wasting any of the fabric; a wider fabric was used for larger sizes. Shirts fit loosely, without any tapering in the body or at the shoulders. They had long, full sleeves eased by gussets under the arms and they opened in a deep slit down the front, with either a band or soft collar that buttoned at the neck.

Wealthy men usually owned enough shirts so they could wear a clean one every day if they so desired. Lord Botetourt, Virginia's royal governor from 1768 to 1770, owned fifty-six ruffled and six plain shirts when the inventory of his estate was taken.

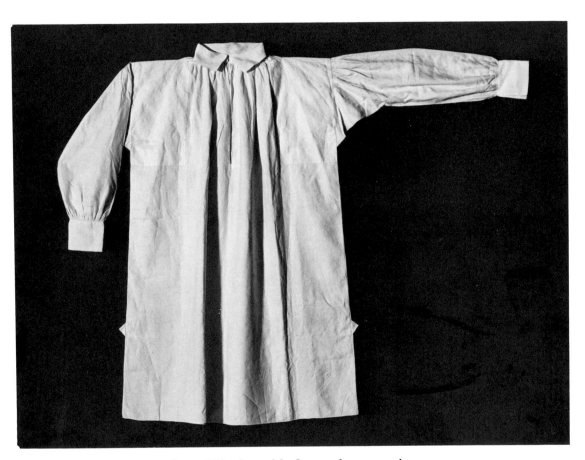

Shirt. White linen woven about 34 inches wide from selvage to selvage, possibly America, 1770-1820. The shirt has a typically generous length of 42½ inches. 1953-967.

D RESS shirts were made of fine bleached linen or cotton and often had ruffles of fine linen or lace attached to the neck opening and at the cuffs. When it was worn with a suit, very little of the dress shirt could actually be seen except for the ruffles, since the stock or cravat, precursors of the modern necktie, fastened around the neck and covered most or all of the shirt's collar.

Shirts worn by working-class men were made of coarser unbleached linens like osnaburg, coarse cottons, and — less often — of checked, striped, or dyed fabrics.

Man and Child Drinking Tea. Artist unknown. Oil on canvas. England, 1720-1730. The man relaxes at home wearing a banyan and cap. His open shirt is held loosely by a ribbon through the buttonholes. 1954-654.

Shirt. White linen with finer linen ruffle, England or America, 1775-1810. The owner's initials W. H. H. are worked in silk cross stitch at the side vent. Anonymous gift, G1971-1552.

B Y 1700 men's suits had assumed the three-piece format still worn in the twentieth century, although the components certainly differed in appearance from today's vested suit. Eighteenth-century suits had long coats, waistcoats that corresponded to the vest and were worn beneath the coat, and knee-length breeches buttoned at the center front. The three parts of the suit, the cut and style of which evolved during the eighteenth century, were not necessarily made of matching colors or fabric.

Coat and Breeches (shown from back; waistcoat missing). Gold silk voided velvet with uncut pile in a lace pattern trimmed with silver galloon and buttons, replaced linings, England, 1735-1745. 1953-836, 1-2.

George Booth as a Young Man by William Dering. Oil on canvas. Virginia,
1740-1750. Booth, who lived in Gloucester County, Virginia, wears the
full-skirted coat and long waistcoat fashionable during the first half of the
eighteenth century. 1975-242.

IN the first half of the eighteenth century, suit coats had full sleeves and wide skirts that ended just below the knee; waistcoats were also long and full and covered most of the breeches. The breeches were styled with gathers at the back, giving extra room in the seat for ease of movement.

Men's suits slowly evolved toward a narrower silhouette with less fullness in the skirts of the coat, shorter waistcoats, and smaller cuffs.

As waistcoats became shorter after mid-century, revealing more of the lower torso, the breeches began to be designed with a flap or "fall" that covered the buttons of the placket to preserve the uninterrupted lines of the suit.

Finer suits were often made of silk fabrics in small-scale repeat patterns woven especially as suiting materials. Many suits were further embellished with applied braid and decorative buttons. Typically, the coat linings were brought directly up to the front edge and sewn in place without using facings.

Suit Coat. Lavender ribbed silk patterned with lozenges and flowers (now faded to pink), replaced linings and buttons, England, 1740-1750. 1954-1056 (reproduction linens).

Suit. Coat, waistcoat, and breeches of matching floral and lozenge silk suiting trimmed with silver gimp and buttons, probably England, 1750-1770. The waistcoat once had removable sleeves (see page 59). 1967-612, 1-3.

Coat and Breeches. Coat, imported uncut and voided silk velvet, originally
bright salmon in color; fall-front breeches, silk twill, originally pinkish
in color, now faded to beige, unlined, England or Virginia, 1750-1770.
Both the velvet coat and silk breeches descended in the Blair-Henderson
family of Virginia and are thought to have been worn by Judge John
Blair. Gift of the Association for the Preservation of Virginia Antiquities,
G1981-180, G1981-183.

Full Dress or Court Suit. Coat and breeches, striped silk embroidered with silk and edged with appliquéd net to represent lace; waistcoat, white ribbed silk with matching embroidery and silk twill back; linings of thin silk twill, napped cotton-linen, and linen, probably France, 1780-1790. 1956-306.

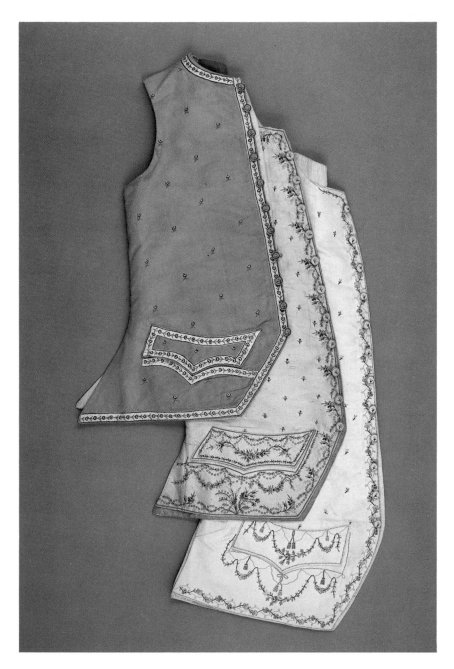

Three Sleeveless Waistcoats. Silk embroidered with tambour work (chain stitch worked with a hook while the fabric is stretched over a frame or round hoop resembling a tambour), backs of undecorated worsted wool, England and France, 1775-1785. 1960-704, 1960-705, 1951-272.

FASHIONABLE waistcoats were often made of elaborate, colorful fabrics brocaded on a loom or hand worked by professional embroiderers. They were available as flat fabric lengths, each of which included all of the decorated shapes necessary to make the fronts of a waistcoat complete to the pocket flaps and circles for covering buttons.

Waistcoat shapes, or patterns as they were often called, were purchased from milliners or other merchants and were taken to a tailor who cut the pieces apart, added extra fabric for back and lining, and sewed the waistcoat to his customer's measurements. Because waistcoats were intended always to be worn under a coat for formal dress, the practical eighteenth-century gentleman did not squander expensive fabric where it could not be seen, and thus usually chose less expensive, plain fabrics for the backs of waistcoats, even in the fanciest suits.

Brodeur. Black and white line engraving. Detail from a plate originally bound in Denis Diderot's *Encyclopédie,* France, ca. 1763. The embroiderers are working on fabric stretched within large frames; the shapes outlined are waistcoat or coat fronts. Anonymous gift, G1971-1934, 2.

Unmade Waistcoat Pattern. Silk woven and brocaded in the shape for waistcoat fronts; below are the pocket flaps and circles to cover the buttons, France, 1780-1795. 1954-284.

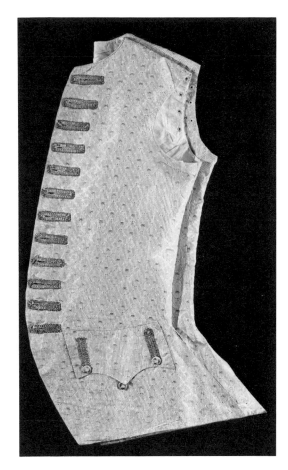

Waistcoat (from suit on page 54). Eyelets worked into the armholes indicate that the waistcoat had removable sleeves at one time. 1967-612.

Sleeved Waistcoat. Linen embellished with cord quilting, French knots, and drawn work (torso shortened and pocket flap moved), England or Continental Europe, ca. 1740. Anonymous gift, G1971-1576.

MEN'S waistcoats were sometimes made with sleeves to provide an additional layer of insulation under the suit coat. Usually the sleeves were sewn in. Occasionally sleeves were tied into place with cords and eyelets so they could be removed.

Although the examples pictured are made of elaborate fabrics, workingmen also wore sleeved waistcoats of sturdy, undecorated materials as a practical solution to the problem of working in cold shops or outdoors. When Alexander Clerk ran away from his master in 1752, he was wearing a blue waistcoat with "large Coat Sleeves to the Waistcoat."[15]

Sleeved Waistcoat (and detail). Green
ribbed silk heavily embroidered with silk
and metallic threads, probably England,
1720-1750. 1967-130.

E LABORATELY embroidered suits were worn by wealthy men on formal occasions, particularly attendance at court. The suits were embroidered to shape by professional needleworkers who produced astonishing, brilliant designs using silk threads, often adding gold, silver, and precious stones — all intended to be visible indicators of the wealth and status of the man wearing the suit, as well as attesting to the importance of the occasion. It was not until the nineteenth century that formal clothing for men substituted dark, conservative colors for the bright hues and elaborate trimmings popular earlier.

Full Dress or Court Coat (and detail). Blue cut silk velvet lavishly embroidered with silk in a floral design, lined with silk, padded and quilted to build out the chest area, France, 1785-1810. Gift of Mr. Mark A. Clark, G1971-433.

Frock Coat. Blue wool broadcloth trimmed with gilt edging, body lining of glazed worsted twill, sleeve linings white linen, England, 1765-1775. 1979-83.

A frock coat had a turn-down collar and a looser fit than a dress coat. It was worn after the second quarter of the eighteenth century for casual occasions and as informal wear in the country. By the 1760s, the frock coat became part of fashionable dress, and it began to be embellished with trimmings and embroidery.

The choice of fabric reflected the less formal nature of the frock, since it was often constructed of wool broadcloth. Frequently referred to simply as "cloth," broadcloth was a wool fabric woven on a wide loom in a plain, or tabby, weave, then fulled to shrink it and give it greater density. After the controlled shrinking, a nap or fuzzy surface was raised by hand

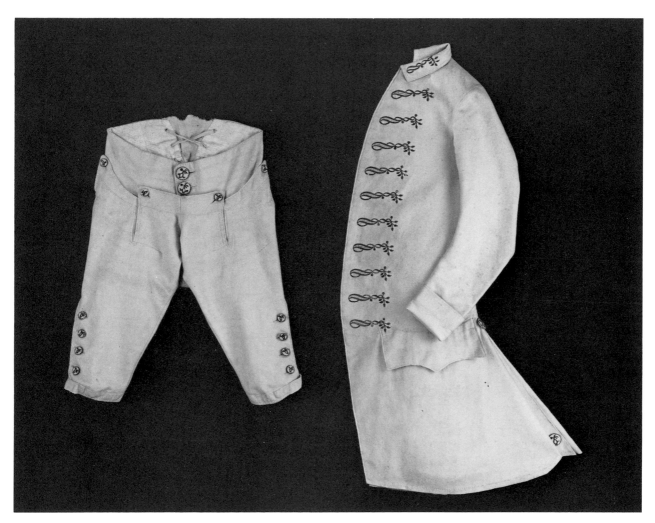

Frock Coat and Matching Breeches (and detail). White wool broadcloth embroidered with metallic silver and sequins, coat body lined with glazed worsted twill, sleeves and breeches lined with napped cotton and linen fustian, England, 1760-1775. 1964-32, 1-2.

Frock coat. Wool broadcloth, lined with silk, worsted and cotton-linen fustian, probably England, 1775-1785. 1983-228.

using an instrument with burr-like teasels that picked and pulled at the fabric, raising the loose fibers. Finally, the fuzzy nap was shorn close to the surface and the fabric was pressed. This process resulted in a textile with a beautiful velvety surface, which was also warm and so dense that it would not ravel when cut.

Clothing made of broadcloth was often constructed without turning up hems or finishing all of the fabric edges. The coats illustrated have hems that have been left raw. The curve of the sleeve over the elbow is characteristic of men's coats of the eighteenth century.

The Honeymoon (detail) by John Collet. Oil on canvas. England, 1755-1765. Relaxing at home, the man wears a frock coat, a cap on his head, an open shirt, and slippers. 1969-48, 3.

WORKINGMEN chose clothing of sturdy fabrics made in ways appropriate to their particular occupations. Frequently they wore aprons over their clothes to protect them from wear and soil. Instead of silk and embroidery, workingmen wore plain, less expensive fabrics: woolens of many types and names, including kersey, plains, "cotton," plaid, bearskin, serge, and broadcloth; coarse linen osnaburg and tow cloth; homespun cottons and linens; and leather, which was made into sturdy breeches for laborers.

Workers' garments often differed in cut from the fashionable ideal. Their coats had roomy sleeves and bodies, giving them more freedom of movement; this is why the comfortable frock coat was often worn by rural and laboring men. Workers in many occupations abandoned the full skirts of the fashionable coat in favor of the shorter jacket, since skirts interfered with easy movement and were hazardous on the job. Sailors and others wore long, loose trousers that ended anywhere from the knee to the ankle and did not have knee bands or cuffs. Some trousers were cut very wide and full at the knee, rather like a modern pair of culottes. Trousers were sometimes layered over knee breeches as a sort of overall. In place of stiff stocks, workingmen wore handkerchiefs around their necks.

Farmers often wore smocks, which were

A Scene near Cox Heath, or the Enraged Farmer (detail). Mezzotint engraving. Printed for R. Sayer and J. Bennett, London, 1779. The English farmer is defending his daughter from the advances of a dandy. He wears a loose smock, breeches, neck handkerchief, and leggings. 1941-224.

much like roomy shirts, over their outer clothing. Evidence suggests that in exceptionally hot weather, field workers occasionally wore smocks or shirts alone while they worked in the fields. Some laborers and explorers wore fabric or leather leggings to protect their lower legs and add warmth.

Some workingmen owned wigs, but they usually wore a soft cap when they were engaged in hard physical labor or they left their own short hair bare. Later in the century, as wigs gradually went out of fashion, workingmen tied their own hair in a tail or queue.

SLAVES' clothing was provided by their masters. The quality depended on the work they were doing as well as on the concern of the slaveowner. Some slaves, particularly household servants, were willed or given used clothing — hand-me-downs. In Virginia, male field slaves appear to have been clothed in a recognizable uniform; advertisements for runaways often implied that the men were attired alike "in the common dress of field slaves."[16] The working suit consisted of a loosely fitting jacket and linen breeches or short trousers for summer and coarse woolens like Kendal cotton, Welsh cotton, and plains for winter. (Although "cotton" meant either a woolen or cotton textile, Kendal and Welsh cottons were actually specific types of woolen cloth during the eighteenth century.) The shirts of field slaves were usually coarse linen osnaburg. Three black men who ran away from a Cumberland County, Virginia, plantation were all clothed in "good white [wool] plains" and "stockings made of the same sort of cloth as their clothes."[17]

Painted Fan (detail; see page 45). The sailors wear jackets, neck handkerchiefs instead of stiff stocks, and striped trousers.
1981-195.

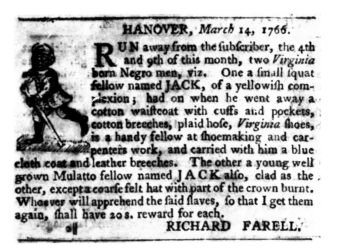

Advertisement for Two Runaway Slaves.
Virginia Gazette (Purdie and Dixon),
March 28, 1766.

Snuff Handkerchief, "Industry and Idleness" (and detail). Plate-printed linen showing moralistic scenes from the lives of good and bad servants, 27 x 30 inches, England, 1770-1785. 1950-104. In the detail, the two men wear loose-fitting jackets; one wears knee breeches and the other ankle-length trousers. Although the handkerchief was printed in England, the garments shown relate closely to those worn by field laborers in Virginia.

Many slaves and some free laborers wore stockings of cut and sewn wool fabrics rather than knitted stockings, which had a tendency to run when snagged. The stockings called "plad" or plaid hose made of a wool fabric called plading were of this style. They were often white rather than being patterned as the word plaid is used today.[18] Many of the textiles worn by servants and slaves in Virginia were cheap grades of woolens and linens made in the British Isles or northern Europe and imported by plantation owners specifically for their slaves' use.

In America as in Europe, male servants to gentry were often provided with suits of livery that were made of good quality wool broadcloth elaborately trimmed with "livery lace" edging the fronts, neck, and cuffs of the coat, and with buttons and trim in a contrasting color taken from the master's coat of arms. Liveried servants also received less fancy everyday clothing to wear when they were not working in public view.

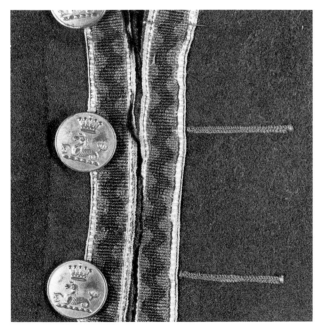

Servant's Livery (and detail). Coat, dark green wool broadcloth with red cuffs and "livery lace," or edge trimming, of uncut velvet, body lining, red worsted twill, linen sleeve linings, England, 1780-1800. Fall front breeches, red wool plush, unlined, England, 1790-1820. 1954-1032, 1954-1035.

URING inclement weather, men wore great coats or long capes called cloaks. They were usually made of wool that was made water repellant by being closely woven and then heavily fulled after weaving. In 1758, Virginian Francis Jerdone ordered a great coat for himself "to fit a man six foot high: I would chuse it to be very warm, and of such substance as will keep out rain for 12 hours."[19]

Robert "King" Carter complained to his English contact about a "fine gay cloke" (that is, a long cape) he had been sent several years before, asserting that it was "fitter for an Alderman of London than a Planter in Virginia. I love plainess and value my cloths more for their use than their finery."[20]

Obviously not every Virginian, even those who could afford it, necessarily dressed flamboyantly. One can detect in the orders and portraits of some Virginia planters a tendency to avoid extremes of fashion and excessive trimmings, while insisting on good quality in materials.

Most methods for keeping warm involved layering: waistcoats with sleeves under suit coats, two pairs of stockings, and wool underwaistcoats with sleeves beneath the other clothing. Landon Carter, however, found problems with his underwaistcoat: "I used to wear my [wool] flannel Waistcoat next to my skin to accommodate the very cold weather of winter. This however produce[d] Vast itching."[21]

Great Coat. Taupe color wool, heavily fulled, unlined, England, 1790-1830. Probably worn by a coachman. 1954-1041.

Cloak. Probably for a man. Red wool, lightly fulled, unlined and unhemmed, possibly New England, second half of the eighteenth century. Gift of Mr. and Mrs. Reginald S. Graves, G1956-213.

Man's Pocketbook. Leather with paper memo book inside and metal pencil, used by William Daniel, England, dated 1777. 1975-129.

R OUNDING out a man's wardrobe were accessories that included hats, caps, gloves, pocketbooks, handkerchiefs, and jewelry. A hat with its brim cocked up on three sides was the most common style of the period for fashionable wear. Uncocked hats were also worn, especially by country men. While working, at home, and on other informal occasions men often wore soft caps of woven or knitted fabrics. When they were not wearing their wigs, caps were particularly useful to men who had shaved heads. Folding pocketbooks that held paper money and bills were carried in the deep pockets of a man's coat or breeches. They could be purchased ready-made in leather and fabric. Women sometimes worked pocketbooks in brilliant wool or silk as gifts. Large handkerchiefs for wiping one's brow, tying about the neck, or sneezing into after a dip of snuff could be purchased plain, checked, or printed.

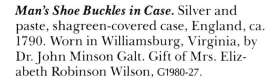

Men's Accessories. Hat, felted fur, linen crown lining, worn in New Hampshire by Josiah Bartlett, probably made in England, 1750-1775. Cap, white cotton and linen embroidered with wool and edged with lace, England, early eighteenth century. Oval snuff box, silver inlaid with mother of pearl and tortoiseshell, England, ca. 1720. Snuff handkerchief, printed linen commemorating Lord George Gordon, England, 1781-1790. Folding pocketbook, wool Irish stitch on canvas, owned by Seth Drew, whose name is worked into the needlework, probably America, dated 1771. Pocket watch, gold, made by George Graham, London, 1750/51. Gloves, leather with silver gilt embroidery, probably England, early eighteenth century. 1960-911, G1971-1374, 1971-240, G1971-1443, 1950-268, 1954-654, 1947-212.

Man's Shoe Buckles in Case. Silver and paste, shagreen-covered case, England, ca. 1790. Worn in Williamsburg, Virginia, by Dr. John Minson Galt. Gift of Mrs. Elizabeth Robinson Wilson, G1980-27.

IN the eighteenth century, children's clothing underwent a gradual evolution from constricting garments patterned after those worn by adults to apparel designed specifically for them. The practice of swaddling infants tightly was gradually discontinued early in the century. Very young children of both sexes wore dresses with close fitting bodices similar to those worn by women. The bodices, which usually fastened at the back, often had leading strings or bands attached to the shoulders to help parents guide a young child who was learning to walk. Perhaps they also acted as a restraint on a lively youngster. Leading strings were occasionally retained on girls' dresses as a symbol of youthfulness long after their practical functions had been outgrown.

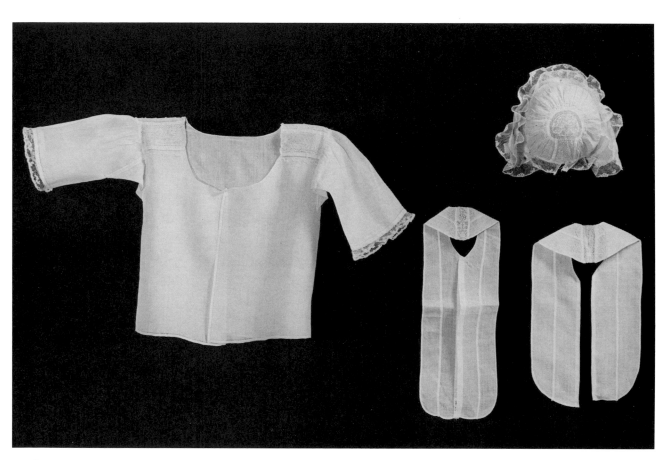

Infant's Linens. Shirt, two neck bands, and cap, fine linen, decorated with "Hollie Point" lace insertions, England, first half of the eighteenth century. 1956-145, G1971-1570, G1971-1572, G1971-1573.

Wishing a Happy New Year to Grand Papa. Black and white mezzotint engraving. Printed for John Bowles, London, 1745-1755. The children wear the formal adult-style clothing and have the posture expected of children during the first half of the eighteenth century; their mother wears a lappet cap and black hooded cloak. 1941-250.

Toddlers sometimes wore padded pudding caps much like modern crash helmets to protect their heads if they fell.

Most small girls and many young boys wore stays, especially with dress clothing, since it was believed that stays supported the back and encouraged proper posture. As late as 1771, Williamsburg milliner Catherine Rathell advertised "thin Bone and Packthread Stays for Children of three Months old and upwards."[22] Not all children, particularly those of the laboring classes, were put in stays, however.

Child's "Pudding" Cap. Quilted cotton velvet bound with silk ribbon, horsehair stuffing, leather lining, probably England, 1770-1785. 1952-55.

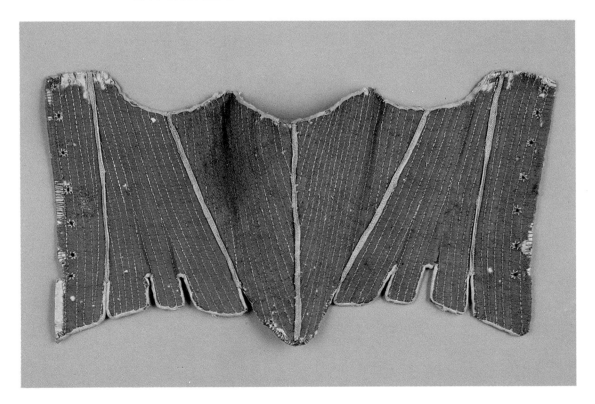

Child's Stays. Green worsted wool satin, boned and lined with linen, with eyelets for lacing up the back, England or America (New York), 1740-1750. The waist measures 17 inches; the center front length measures 7½ inches. 1964-405.

Portrait of Two Children
attributed to Joseph Badger. Oil
on canvas. America, mid-eighteenth century. The boy at the left
is wearing a frock similar to that
shown below. Abby Aldrich
Rockefeller Folk Art Center,
57.100.15.

Boy's Frock or Gown. Striped coral
and green silk and linen, bodice
and sleeves lined with linen, probably England, 1740-1750. The
waist measures 20 inches and the
overall length is 27 inches. 1952-335.

A philosophical movement toward less restrictive dress for children occurred during the second half of the eighteenth century, and by 1760 the already well-established fashion was for little boys and girls to wear white dresses called frocks that had sashes at the waist. Late in the 1700s, boys began to wear suits with long trousers rather than knee breeches, a fashion that won favor about twenty years before it was accepted by adult men for dress wear. Throughout the century, the time when a little boy went from skirts to pants, which was called "breeching," occurred anytime from age three to seven and was symbolic of his first step toward becoming a "little man."

Children in a Classroom. Sepia aquatint with stipple. Drawn by T. Stothard, engraved by C. Knight, England, ca. 1790. The children wear the clothing of the late eighteenth century — frock dresses for the girls and trouser suits for the boys. The engraver suggests society's evolving attitude toward children by their lively postures and more comfortable clothing. Anonymous gift, G1971-3139.

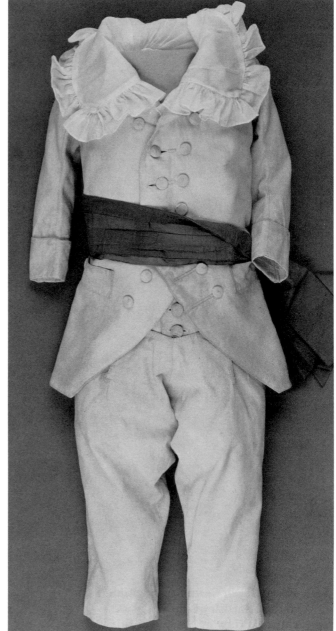

Boy's Suit. White cotton coat and trousers, lined with linen, England, 1785-1795. 1953-841 (reproduction shirt and sash).

Child's Shoes. Dark brown leather, 6 inches long, probably Europe, 1730-1750. 1985-235, 1-2.

Girl's Shoes. Buff leather with striped linen lining, 6¾ inches long with a 2-inch heel, possibly America, ca. 1760. 1953-1043.

Young Boy in Green Suit attributed to the Beardsley Limner. Oil on canvas. Probably New England, ca. 1790. The boy wears the suit and shirt with large open collar fashionable at the time. Abby Aldrich Rockefeller Folk Art Center, 64.100.4.

Footnotes

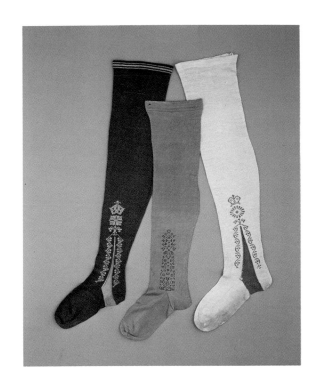

1. "Letters of Rev. Jonathan Boucher," *Maryland Historical Magazine,* VII (1912), p. 5.

2. Gregory A. Stiverson and Patrick H. Butler III, eds., "Virginia in 1732: The Travel Journal of William Hugh Grove," *Virginia Magazine of History and Biography,* LXXXV (1977), p. 29.

3. Stephen Hawtrey to Edward Hawtrey, Mar. 26, 1765, Alumni File, College Archives, Earl Gregg Swem Library, College of William and Mary, Williamsburg, Va.

4. Diary of Sarah Fouace Nourse, Berkeley County, Virginia, July 8, 1781, Alderman Library, University of Virginia, Charlottesville, Va. Typescript in the Research Library, Colonial Williamsburg Foundation, Williamsburg.

5. Frances Norton Mason, ed., *John Norton & Sons, Merchants of London and Virginia* (Richmond, Va., 1937), p. 331.

6. For a full discussion of short gowns and jackets, see Claudia Kidwell, "Short Gowns," in *Dress,* IV (1978), pp. 30-61.

7. *Virginia Gazette* (Purdie and Dixon), Feb. 5, 1767.

8. *Ibid.* (Hunter), Sept. 29, July 3, 1752.

9. *Ibid.* (Rind), Dec. 14, 1769.

10. Neil McKendrick, John Brewer, and J. H. Plumb, *The Birth of a Consumer Society* (Bloomington, Ind., 1982).

11. Hunter Dickinson Farish, ed., *Journal & Letters of Philip Vickers Fithian, 1773-1774: A Plantation Tutor of the Old Dominion* (Williamsburg, Va., 1957), p. 29.

12. *The Spectator,* June 27, 1711, no. 102.

13. Norton, ed., *John Norton & Sons,* p. 66.

14. Farish, ed., *Journal of Fithian,* p. 150.

15. *Virginia Gazette,* Apr. 10, 1752.

16. *Ibid.* (Purdie and Dixon), Dec. 13, 1770.

17. *Ibid.,* Feb. 9, 1769.

18. I am indebted to Helen Bennett for confirming my suspicion that plaid hose were, indeed, made of cut and sewn fabric.

19. Letter Book of Francis Jerdone, February 1758, Swem Library.

20. Victor Dennis Golloday, "The Nicholas Family in Virginia, 1722-1780" (Ph.D. diss., University of Virginia, 1973), p. 53.

21. Jack P. Greene, ed., *The Diary of Colonel Landon Carter of Sabine Hall, 1752-1778,* II (Charlottesville, Va., 1965), p. 902.

22. *Virginia Gazette* (Purdie and Dixon), Oct. 10, 1771.